The Last Words

Will Be Spoken...

A Journey Into the Thoughts
and Rhymes of A Poetic Mind

Brandan

"BStuc ThaPoet"

Stuckey

authorHOUSE®

AuthorHouse™
1663 Liberty Drive
Bloomington, IN 47403
www.authorhouse.com
Phone: 1-800-839-8640

First published by AuthorHouse 6/14/2010

ISBN: 978-1-4520-2594-0 (e)
ISBN: 978-1-4520-2596-4 (sc)

Library of Congress Control Number: 2010907758

Printed in the United States of America
Bloomington, Indiana

This book is printed on acid-free paper.

Dedicated to
the Mic and the Stage
the Pen and the Page

Table of Contents

PILOT EPISODE Introduction...ix

SEASON 1 What's In A Name...1

    Episode I   My Name Is My Name 3

    Episode II   People Say...5

    Episode III Target...7

    Episode IV A Poem For Omega 11

    Episode V   The Bestus...15

SEASON 2 Obama! We Did It!...19

    Episode I   We Did It! 21

SEASON 3 "Love Ain't No Joke"..25

    Episode I   Mi Chica De Negra...27

    Episode II   Comic Book Lover...29

    Episode III Let Me Hold You 31

    Episode IV Championship...34

    Episode V   Contagious 37

    Episode VI Breaking Up...40

    Episode VII Loved and Lost 42

    Episode VIII Love's Assassin...44

    Episode IX Pray For H.E.R. 47

    Episode X   Sunshine's Goodnight (The Morning).........................49

    Episode XI Waiting..52

Season 4 I Go Through It, Sometimes! 55

   Episode I We Must Become Firemen...57

   Episode II 2 Weeks Notice...60

   Episode III Protect and Serve...63

   Episode IV The Lion's Den...68

   Episode V At The End Of The Day: (Love vs. Money) 71

   Episode VI "iGrow"...73

   Episode VII The Storm of 5/1/09..75

Season 5 The Paternity Journey 79

   Episode I Act I..81

   Episode II Act II...83

   Episode III Act III..85

Series Finale The Conclusion 87

Introduction

If poetry is life then life is poetry. On your death bed would you prefer your last words be read or spoken? The journey for the answer to this question began as a burgeoning college student. I often clashed with my poetry professor over the written form of poetry versus the verbal contemporary version known as Spoken word. With little to no regard of its value, my professor quickly deemed Spoken word as ranting. One thing I don't do is rant! If I could, I'd go back in time and pose this very serious question to her. Would you prefer your last words be read or would you prefer to enunciate your feelings, your final transcript in life, to forever convey a message into the ears of the attentive? I honor the literary contributions of Langston Hughes, Walt Whitman, Nikki Giovanni, Emily Dickinson, and others. Their words have been read by many. However, I want my words, my thoughts, my ideas, my poems, to be spoken to the generations who have yet to be heard. I want to lend a voice to the voiceless. I hope to give a stage to the stage less. I wish to speak life to the lifeless. Indeed, the last words will be spoken.

I apologize for the length of time it's taken to get to this point. Can you believe it's been ten years since I wrote my first poem for my high school black history play? I knew from the crowd's reaction that this was the beginning of something special. God, in his infinite wisdom, saw fit to allow me this opportunity to express myself to the masses.

I remember the first time I heard Snoop Dogg rap, "With so much drama in the LBC, it's kinda hard being Snoop D-O double G." It awakened a dormant spirit in me. I was around the age of 12 or 13. Until then, I'd only been exposed to MC Hammer and the New Jersey Mass Choir. It's an interesting mix of music, I know! Many of our tests in life and the parameters in which we use to pass those tests can be linked to the drama in the LBC. I don't mean the physical Long Beach, CA. But the LBC can be our jobs, church, family, friends, or school. In those aforementioned places, it can be very easy to lose yourself. As an artist, redundancy has plagued our world of creativity. Many artists have allowed their art to be compromised by unappreciative forces that seek to get all they can and can all they get. Rather than allow my work to be classified as ranting or be shaped by the image of others, I set out to make my own definition. Hopefully, this work will be classified among the greats, who themselves sought to express their feelings and emotions in order to change the world before them.

All of the questions that have plagued scholars when analyzing a contemporary poet's work will be answered in my book. This work will document detailed thoughts and experiences that I encountered when writing. I have a myriad of obstacles that I've had to overcome that would have turned out differently had I not been given the power of the pen. One instance in particular involved a verbal disagreement between me and a former employee. I'd mapped out in my mind how hard I would strike this person. They were gonna feel my wrath! I even planned other things to do with my life just in case things didn't go according to plan. I had a lawyer on stand-by and a bail bondsman on 2-Way. The situation was heavy to say the least. This person's life was in danger because they were blinded by their own conscious and pompous ego. Thank God for this precious gift of poetry that provided rhetorical restraint. For if it had not been for His grace and guidance to remind me of my gifts, I would not be here communicating with you, my precious supporter.

Since I'm a product of the Hip-Hop Generation, I must take time to acknowledge my favorite artists that helped shape me as a poet. I'm an avid follower of the music from the members of the Dungeon Family. As a matter of fact, I pay homage to OutKast, Cee-Lo, and the Late Great Notorious B.I.G. for their soulful contributions that continue to stand the test of time. *Life After Death, SpeakerBoxxx/Love Below, B.o.B vs. Bobby Ray, Cee-Lo Green and his Perfect Imperfections*, are some of the albums I had on repeat during the writing of this book. With that being said, I now invite you into the meticulous creative world of a Spoken word poet. Let's delve into this poetic therapy. Enjoy!

"What's In A Name?"

My Name Is My Name

I…B,,,Stuc…In your mind for an appointed time
Played out in a sequence of divine design I commit crimes
Against the alphabet, I'm a mass manipulator of words
Crowds gather 'round for a taste of my verbs
My pronouns are so profound
My words resound with that tinkling cymbal sound
I rearrange letters
I can take the word cold and turn it into a sweater
BStuc is the definition
I'm the premonition that's embedded in your dreams
I'm the substance of things hoped for, evidence not seen
Have faith in me
I'm an instrument played by God so faithfully
The least I can do is recite in this mic so gratefully
'Cause He's been great to me
I speak life into a mic to a world so ill
My name is my name like Marlo Stanfield
Avon Barksdale, I spit it through *The Wire*
I prayed that my name would define inspire
All I had to do is stick with it
Now I'm a part of a golden ticket
The scary thing about is I'm only the Vice-president
I stand here before you while He sets the precedent
It became evident that I'm more than Neo-Soul
I'm unraveling the matrix using one neo's soul
I've already told you what I'd do to the cold

And I won't stop until my streets are paved in gold
So the name BStuc is synonymous with crime
And you all are now victims of Black on Black rhyme!

Did you catch that last line? That last line was in reference to my Black on Black Rhyme poetry family when I was living in Tallahassee, FL. Your name is your reputation and your reputation precedes your accomplishments. Which is why Marlo Stanfield, a popular character on the HBO hit series The Wire played by Jamie Hector, worked so hard to ensure his name had value within the community. In an episode of Season 5, he bellowed to his cohorts that "my name is my name!" Although the things he participated in were illegal and morally reprehensible, I identified with his passionate plea to keep the value and merit of his name. The name BStuc represents an acronym meaning to Boldly Stay Tough Under Circumstances. The circumstances that I've encountered have been tough, tenacious, but in the end triumphant. Psalm 37 says the steps of good man are ordered by the Lord. This means that all of your goals in life are there for the taking but the path you take won't necessarily be smooth. Staying tough is the only option because what's on the other side of the struggle is beautiful. No matter what you encounter in life, your temperament and demeanor will determine your outcome. My life experiences have made me and shaped me. I've been given strength and wisdom to overcome whatever is thrown at me. However, my name wouldn't mean anything if I hadn't had God on my side through it all. So I write and recite this poem not only to shed light on my many attributes but to pay homage to what God has done for me and continues to bring me through.

People Say

People say when I speak
All I'm missing is a bowtie and bean pies
My replies are often that of chastise
Cause I despise when my ideas are demonized
It makes me wonder if you're looking at me through demon eyes
I'd like to be cheerful but I got teary eyes
Cause my people be not wise
So my forecast calls for dark and dreary skies
With a chance for more and more compounding lies
An ongoing cycle of this Crimson tide
Seems like we'en been right since 'Pac died
Or since they changed Mamas on Fresh Prince
I'm convinced and incensed that this crab theory leaves us dense
So we cannot rise
Trying to break this glass ceiling
But we running out of tries
People say when I speak
I add value to shock
I get you high when you low like when crack rock
Hit the docks and then the block
Now we just ticks with no tock
With rims that spin counter clock
That runs in place until time stops
Still picking cotton at clothing shops
Just to receive insecure props
They kill me with their kindness

5

Our downfall may be our blindness
Won't get the message if its rhymeless
So we bask in a light that's limeless
So in my pursuit to be your highness
People say I speak that truth that fire that's timeless

I'm sort of a mixed bag. Being a true Gemini has caused me to be labeled by some as the greatest person to be around and others can't stand me. I guess that's life. But one thing is universal about my demeanor is that I say what I mean and mean what I say. This mantra is seen in several of my pieces. So many people would come up to me after a show and tell me how inspired they were after hearing my poetry. I try to write pieces that are profound but I seek a common touch that connects with everyone's personal struggle. I say things that community leaders neglect to say. With words, I paint a vivid picture of reality absent from syntax. With every performance, I try to become the leader that's needed but not described. So many so called leaders talk loud and don't say anything. Most of their verbiage is filled with holes and broken promises. I hope that over time, my words and my leadership becomes inundated with vision, virility, and vigor.

Target

You've made yourself a *Target* in the middle of *Wal-Mart*
Vendors coming at you trying to pick you apart
Trying to stay sane is the price of fame
But overcoming adversity is the key to the game
Maintain some longevity or be a flash in the pan
How you plant your feet will set your worth as a man
Bloom where you're planted and watch your access be granted
Code your actions and your speech and haters won't understand it
You've been here before the outcome is glorious
Even if you die, you'll live on like Notorious
BIG you're larger than life plus the strife
Gives you something deep when you step up to the mic
Cause somebody's got to die
They flow, you gotta flow
Pens bleed just like us
Step on stage and just go
Throw that weight off your shoulder
Make your words sound colder
You're on another level
You can move boulders

Moving mountains like Raymond
Change your life like Namand
Brice from *The Wire*
Spit to inspire
Spit with desire
Spit with perspire
Spit before you expire
Spit to retire
I command you to live long
Been framed as the villain for so long but stay strong
Even the villain made it to the top as King Kong
So do whatever it takes to get to the spot where you belong
Before shows end, and God breaks out His gong
I hope you do something great like the wall in Hong Kong
Losing is not an option and neither is failure
Be brave and await whatever dangers assail you
Use discipline and direction to do what's right
May God give you His strength and His will to fight
And do it all for His glory
This is my version of a champion's story

Whenever I do this piece and I belt out the first line, "You've made yourself a Target in the middle of Wal-Mart," the crowds unanimously shift their body position and lend a keen ear to the words I spit. I wrote *Target* after I participated in *Southern Fried Poetry Slam 2008* in Tallahassee, FL. It was one of the best experiences, as poet, I ever had. There were close to 200 poets from various cities across the country. The competition was fierce. Poets shared in the triumphs of victory and the agony of defeat. Several young poets shared discouraging demeanors after valiant efforts fell short of the mark. Suffering a loss of any aspect is tough to handle. Dr. Martin Luther King, Jr. said "the ultimate measure of a man is not where he stands in moments of comfort and convenience, but where he stands in times of challenge and controversy." This quote displays the underlying theme of *Target*. I hope this poem provides the definitive characteristics to those in need of encouragement and strength to continue their journey. As a young, professional, college graduate, there is a target on me and others like me that I fear may never go away. We must learn to embrace this target rather than fear it. The thrill of the journey is that we know that bullets will assail us daily but will not penetrate because of the protection God provides.

Ω A Poem for Omega Ω

Stony the road we trod
Bitter the chastening rod
For our prayers to God
Were granted with a simple nod
As we face the dawn of 100 years
And celebrate the advances of 3 Musketeers
Where 2 or 3 gathers God is in the midst
Well 3 gathered but it took 4 to complete this
Mission of men
In hopes to become better men
The Bishop, The Professor, The Doctor, and The Biologist
Gave birth to an organization of actors, athletes,
astronauts, poets, and psychologists
Brothers from all walks
Run without weary
Crossing sands in different lands
Eyes get teary
From the Alpha chapter to Zeta Kappa
Christian men of intellect and enthusiasm
Building bridges for one another to cross life's chasms
Though our path is rough and beset by shards
Don't forget in conflict to stand on your cards
Manhood first, Scholarship comes next
Perseverance and Uplift ends the text
But it starts the hearts of men so true
Our vision and virtue allows us to "See It Through"

So stand my brother
Let our light so shine
My hand in your hand
Lifting as we climb
For the bridge that's built
Only costs one toll
That your friendship be essential to the soul
Through recession, oppression, and learning life's lessons
We must continue in thy duty and seek God's blessings
The faith of our friendship
And the bond of this fraternity
Unites us in brotherhood
That lasts an eternity
Refuse to lose
On the path in life you choose
From 1911 to heaven
Long Live The Ques!!!

Long live the Ques indeed. The legend of this band of brothers continues to grow. When James Weldon Johnson wrote *Lift Every Voice And Sing,* he created an anthem for African Americans that is heralded through our continuous accomplishments. "Stony the road we trod, bitter the chastening rod," not only extrapolates the Black struggle but it conceptualizes the encounter that the founders and members of this fraternity face. Every year, thousands of young men enter into the sacred folds of Omega. It only took three undergraduate students and one faculty advisor on the campus of Howard University to change the course of history for black men in the United States. Bishop Edgar A. Love, Professor Frank Coleman, Dr. Oscar J. Cooper, and Dr. Ernest Just founded the Omega Psi Phi Fraternity on November 17, 1911. As a member of this mighty fine organization, I join the thousands of brothers who celebrate their service and duty daily. It is with tremendous honor and great privilege that I take time out and craft these words of literary expression to convey how I feel about this organization. These four men created an institution that has taken men of high esteem and done the impossible by making those men greater. One of those men was the late Bro. Julius Roberson. He was initiated in the Nu Epsilon chapter at Alabama A&M in 1969. I came to know this brother as an undergraduate at the University of South Alabama at a time where I sought to change the world as I see it. While attending the Greater Mount Olive Baptist Church #2 in Mobile, AL, I gained his friendship. He was the chairman of the Sunday school and very involved in the welfare of the children and young adults of the church. He got me involved in several church activities. He regularly called upon me to review the Sunday school lesson. In doing so, his request for me to speak served as practice and preparation for many soon to come performances. I learned how to think on my feet because sometimes I wouldn't know what the lesson was about but the audience never knew the difference. Bro. Roberson awakened something in my spirit and character that needed to be brought out. He'd always recall the lesson learned from *Bridge Builder*, a poem by Will A. Dromgoole that serves as a very important theme to Omega men. He'd remind me that one day I would have to become a bridge builder. Shortly after I moved to Florida, I found out he passed away. I was deeply saddened. However his loss on earth is God's gain in heaven. I'm sure he's serving a larger and very important purpose in the army of the Lord. His passing let me know that it is my turn to help brothers avoid the pitfalls in life that seek to alter the course of so many. Essentially this is what the Omega Psi Phi Fraternity, Inc. is all about. Lifting as we climb has allowed us to span the test of time. Omega Psi Phi 'til the day, the day, that I die!

The Beetus

Clouds gather over
To symbolize the easy part's over
The darkest October
Oh how I long to feel sober
Lady luck moves further and further away from my shoulder
Never been colder
Laying on this bathroom floor dying
Hard to persevere when my eyes are crying
Tears well Tears spell
A gateway to my soul that burns like hell
I hope God is prying
Deep within my body to find a pancreas
Yearning
Begging
Trying
To pump pump
So criss-crossed
I jump jump
Used to be large like Klump Klump
Now I'm small like stump stump
Damn, I could really kick myself
Choices in my diet has me 'bout to stick myself
For accuracy in my reading I have to prick myself
To think it's all good better not trick myself
Every day is a drag
Passed down to me from my Dad and Dad's Dad

Glad
That it wasn't something else
Something worse
Feeling nothings left
But I keep shooting
Like a fan in the stands
For myself I keep rooting
Every time I eat
Feels like I'm polluting
Freedom isn't free
In this war I keep booting
Type 1 or Type 2
Doctors aren't sure
If only there was a cure
A heart once pure
Struggles to endure
As I lay here dying
Members of the family stand 'round crying
As gears shift mind drifts
To thoughts 'bout Lion
My transition from Simba to an eagle that's flying
Has reached a point to where there is no shying
With God's grace in this race I hope I won't end up tying
Cause I'm a winner in whatever I'm vying
Feels so contrary to how they find my lying
Get up BStuc, Keep fighting!

Former World Heavyweight Boxing Champion Mike Tyson once said that everyone has a plan until they get punched in the face. In October of 2006, a sweet haymaker connected with a body shot that had me down for the count. I was rendered inanimate on the bathroom floor of my grandparents' house. It had been a year since doctors at the University of South Alabama told me I was at risk for Diabetes. They prescribed preventative medication for me and I was placed on a strict exercise and diet program. After months of treatment, I felt good. I looked good. Everything was good. Fast forward to now, my body was shutting down. The weight loss I experienced from diet and exercise was replaced by unexplained and uncontrolled weight loss. I looked good but I felt awful. The funny thing about it was no matter how much weight I lost, my head remained the largest in the world! Anyway, lying on that cold floor taught me three things. One was that I had been misdiagnosed as a Type II diabetic. The preventative and substantive medication I had been given served little to no consequence in improving my overall heath. I was actually a Type I and I'd been experiencing something known as the "honeymoon phase." It's when your body doesn't feel any adverse effects from the disease for a significant period of time. But once it's over you feel it in a major way! This explained why I was rendered motionless. My mouth was tasteless. My body was every word that could fit with the suffix –less. Two was that I couldn't continue to leave my health in the hands of so called health professionals. Their failure to see my body's deterioration only contributed to vital miscues in treatment. One of the medicines I was prescribed has been subsequently taken off the market because it was literally killing people. I was left with a feeling of disenchantment. Finally, the third thing I learned was that as soon as I felt better, I needed to mop that floor! I was taken to the hospital and pumped with two IV's and insulin from an exogenous source. My road to recovery has been a test of endurance and perseverance. I felt better but not

100 percent. Slowly, I regained my strength. My breaking point came when I met with a diabetic counselor. She prepared me for the mental aspect and the responsibility that I had to maintain my health. It was at that moment that I knew this was real. I had met a wall and my life depended on climbing and getting on the other side of it. There was no turning back. I put on my boots, grabbed my rope, and hoisted myself up and over. The biggest adjustment for me was maintaining a sense of privacy with a public disease. People need to know that a family member, coworker, or best friend has diabetes. I strongly encourage these individuals to "properly" educate themselves and become aware of what diabetes is and what it does to the people that are afflicted. I have an idea that will revolutionize the diabetic community. I am in the process of establishing a non profit organization that tackles diabetes head on. The BSTUC Foundation is devoted to achieving victory over diabetes through advocacy, education, research, and service. We are deeply rooted in Habakkuk minded planning, preparation, prosperity. The Foundation believes in writing the vision for success in every endeavor, so that at an appointed time, our character, commitment, and conquest will be honored. To all my readers, help me lead a grass roots effort to combat this disease. Send your stories to bstucthapoet@ gmail.com and your voice will be heard on the all new website www. thebstucfoundation.org. Keep Fighting!

Obama! We Did It!

We Did It!

We Did It! If anybody was scared, they hid it
After decades of injustice in this country, we rid it!
We run the city like Diddy did it!
In the streets yelling, "Yes We Can!"
Going uptown like we trying to make the band
But this prize is far too great for mere cheesecake
So we'll take the whole plate
Cause we're gonna need that fuel
Been denied for so long of our 40 acres and mule
So we took 50 states and a White House
I'm not talking history, this is right now
We Did It!
And got change back
That was more than 50 cent
We don't have to be a rapper or an actor
Let's strive to be evident
Let's seek better residence
Use God as our evidence
And the reward A Black President!
Refuse limitation
Accept liberation
Awaken from the dream
So fresh and so clean
No longer are we outcast
We outlast the struggles of the past
The aftermath of that ballot cast
Helped pick democracy out the trash
Where it resided for the last 8 years
So celebrate with cheers and tears
'Cause for one night, one man, one God, calmed all our fears
And we look back on the progress of the Holy Spirit
And claim loudly, We Did It!
Who Did it?
We Did it!

We've gone from "Keep Hope Alive" to "Yes We Can" and now we can all say "We Did It!" What a joyous occasion this election turned out to be! It wasn't until after writing this poem that I was given the moniker "The Presidential Poet." I lived in Florida at the time. It's funny how the state once mired in controversy over the election of George W. Bush returned eight years later with a crushing victory for our 44th President Barack Obama. I participated for the first time as an early voter. This was a spirited occasion for me because I was used to standing in long voter lines in the state of Alabama's fossilized voting process. I wasn't accustomed to a less than minute procedure. So I and a coworker voted 2 weeks before the historic day of Nov. 4, 2009. There was an old man in the voting line behind me. He was so ecstatic to see me and my friend in line to vote. "I'm so proud to see you youngsters getting out to vote," he exclaimed. "When I was yo' age dey ain't want us to be out here talking 'bout no vote'n!," he continued. "We were hit in da head wit rocks, bricks, keys, and anything they could grab!" Until this point, I hadn't realized the generational impact of President Obama's run for office. It's easy to compartmentalize his victory as the first American president not of European ancestry. However, the election of our first African American president meant so much more. To me and my generation it was an expected occurrence that would happen sooner than later. Obama's historic win was rooted in faith and a belief that a change would come and that change would occur in our lifetime. The 18-30 demographic led the fight to get President Obama elected. College kids across the country led grass roots efforts on behalf of the former Senator from Illinois. As a student, I often wondered what my place in history would've been had I sat next to Rosa Parks or stood in the powerful stream of firemen's hoses in Selma, AL. President Obama's election made me wonder no more. The measures that were taken to ensure victory removes the negative stereotypes surrounding Generation X and Y, and placed us on the forefront of history. This is the beginning of a new era. To past generations, it meant the fulfillment of hope through a dark cloud of injustice from an endless storm of oppression. The statements made by the elder gentleman in the voting line reflected the dimmed optimism of a seemingly failed generation. To know that all of the marches, bloodshed, dogs, and fire hoses, were not in vain became an awe-inspiring thrill for him and his fellow members of the civil rights generation. I was inspired to write this poem on Nov. 5, 2009 after attending a Wednesday night prayer service at the Bethel Missionary Baptist Church in Tallahassee, FL. Everyone adorned their Barack Obama attire. There were hats, T-shirts, church fans, and buttons peppered throughout the congregation. Sidebar: To this day, I feel I am the only one in my generation that doesn't own a Barack Obama T-Shirt. A rejuvenated spirit of joy and elation took over the church. There were high fives, hand claps, and the most beautiful Colgate smiles you could find. The lady sitting next to me shouted, "We did it!" She had no idea that her exclamation provided the impetus for the words expressed in this poem.

"Love Ain't No Joke"

Mi Chica De Negra

Only one such being inhabits Mother Earth
Capable of bringing excellence through the stresses of child birth
Beautiful you are like a shining star you twinkle
As you enter my mind love begins to sprinkle
Clandestine thoughts of eternal bliss
Exploring your erogenous zones to that I add a kiss
But it seems as if our relationship cannot withstand
The vile and wretched pressures of this land
Though this moment of love was very much needed
I'm ashamed at the moments that just preceded
I hate to fight before we make love
We shouldn't be together if we result to matches of push and shove
Your flippant outbursts followed by the most foulest of language
Does not justify the love I give for me to feel so much anguish
Despite our adversity you still occupy my heart
No matter how rough the road it will never depart
Because I'm infatuated with your breasts and the lust of your lips
And I take pride in the notion that I help add to your hips
But the thing that reaches out captures my affection
That surpasses your complexion bringing my member to erection
Lies atop your temple, above your eyes, lies your mind
Where I become perplexed or perhaps intertwined
Into late night conversations of love on the phone
Kinda like Nia Long and Larenz Tate
I have a love jones for your body and a your skin tone
Mi Chica De Negra, My Woman of Blackness

How is it through the years you stay so attractive
Rise above insecurities and stay true to yourself
Because what you bring to me accumulates more than wealth
It adds to my health a life of long lasting
Mi Chica De Negra bringing me so much passion

I wrote this poem my freshman year at the University of South Alabama. The first girl I met there was this beautiful mocha covered goddess. She spoke Spanish fluently and I wanted to impress her. So I entered into a poetry slam on campus and crafted these words. I actually have this on video somewhere. At the time, I hadn't really made a name for myself other than being the only person on campus with locs. This night was my grand introduction to the campus. It was a packed house. South was a commuter school. Many events on campus were heavily attended by students that stayed in the campus dorms. As a matter of fact, the event was co-sponsored by one of the student organizations in which she was a member. So, chances were good that she'd be there. Ten other poets were ahead of me talking about everything from politics, education, and even pet ownership. When the numbers slowly crept towards me, I started to get cold feet. Before I reached a level where I memorized and actually performed poetry, I would go on stage and read from a steno pad. There I was in front of a room full of students. I was so nervous. I said "this is a collection of thought and feelings that come to mind when I think about a black woman." The ladies went crazy! Each line built anticipation for the next. By poems end, I managed to galvanize the ladies to not only feel good about themselves, but to also feel good to know there were some good brothers left out here. The highlight of the night was when the poem manifested itself as I left the show hand in hand with *Mi Chica De Negra.*

Comic Book Lover

Behold a lady
I knew she'd be my baby
The day I went crazy and jumped off a cliff
Believing I could fly because she made me feel like Superman
She brought out the Super in this man
When I'm normally Clark Kent
Shy and hiding in a phone booth
Acting reckless and uncouth
Until she hits me with her lasso of truth
What a wonderful woman, better yet, be my Wonder Woman
And we form our own Justus League
Get it the "Just-Us" League
How about we trek the seven seas
Or explore different galaxies
How about we make Super Hero love with no fatigue
Does that peak your intrigue?
Let's take to the skies as caped crusaders
Warding off invaders and "Starscream-like" playa-haters
I'm glad it was I you chose,
We make a good team fighting off these nappy headed foes
Let's slide past the adversity
Because you still remain first to me
And anything less would be a curse to me
So please accept this verse from me
And give me a moment to behold you my lady, my baby,
my comic book love

With this poem, I wanted to use a lot of imagery. I had a beautiful young lady that I was dating who made me feel good. I started writing this poem in the spring of 2007. It was right before the summer movie season and right after Don Imus made a few off color remarks about the Rutgers University women's basketball team. The morale for black women had hit a low point. I even noticed the woman that I loved had an insecure smile upon her face. I knew I couldn't touch every black woman in America but I could at least bring about the passion and desire that made my queen so special. So like any other poet, I picked up my pen to write. The best lovers have an uncanny ability to accentuate the gifts and talents of their mates. The goal of any relationship should be to form a bond with enough strength to overcome the limits that the sky beholds. The line, "Shy and hiding in a phone booth acting reckless and uncouth," highlights traits that are unbecoming to a successful relationship. It takes a special woman, a "wonder woman," to bring out the "Super" in a man.

Let Me Hold You

(The first two lines and the last two lines are sung in the tune of
Luther Vandross' *If Only For One Night*)

Let me hold you tight
If only for one night
Just leave me with the satisfaction
That we gave this chemistry traction
As we mix an intoxicating potion
Of you, I, and this bottle of emotion
Your neck, becomes so inviting
Coupled with, supple hips
Under Harvest Moon lighting
And with the harvest comes the feast
You provide a mixture of love's elixir
That soothes the savage beast
The good times keeps us going
The bad times makes us stronger
I'm gonna close my eyes
And hold you tight and make my time last longer
They say beauty is in the eye of the beholder
But beauty is in my arms as I hold her

Hold you, take hold of you
As we catapult to heights up above
Twinkle, twinkle, we shine like little stars in a play called Love
If….love is a drug
Wait….love is a drug
Whether inhaled or shot through the veins
This is the free health care that politicians lie about in their campaigns
When all the world is fearful and hiding under a rug
I'm in a corner somewhere, overdosed on your hug
They say, life is hard by the yard
But it's a cinch by the inch
I say life is long and you need that inner strength
To go that extra length
To go that extra mile
I'm captivated by your touch
I'm motivated by your smile
As the sun begins to rise
And dusk turns into dawn
And we await the new day
And whatever trials may spawn
I hope I make it through the wrongs
To what just feels so right
I thank you for this moment that you….
Let me hold you tight

Ladies and gentlemen, I proudly present my signature poem. From old to young, black to white, rich to poor, this poem always garners overwhelming support. The raw emotions that the words of this piece bring out are uncanny and unique in its own right. My only regret is that the great talent, Luther Vandross, is no longer with us to hear his legendary song transformed into a spoken word piece. With this poem, I sought to create an atmosphere of intimacy unabashed to the counter-productive measures that seek to dim love's light. So many young couples fall victim to overcomplicating love. Some copy the success of their friends' relationships. Others resort to displaying their affections through new technological tactics that social networks like Facebook and MySpace provide. However, love is very simple. In order to reap the full benefits of love, you must have intimacy. To me, there's nothing more intimate than lying in a hammock on a cool summer night under God's pale moon light with the one you love. These precious moments provide an escape from the hassles of life and usher in the sweet bliss of love's caress. *Let Me Hold You* also provides one of love's noted attributes. The couple in this piece enjoyed each other's company without being cognizant of time. They were able to savor the flavor of the sunset and embrace the skies of sunrise. There's nothing more intimate than that!

Championship

Whenever you're ready to stop running
Baby...I'll be here gunning
For the championship
Where champions sit...and sip the finest
Where I'm known as your highness his flyness
Stuc, B, the motto
The scene is the grotto
Where we cool our jets we soaking wet
'Bout to do some things we won't regret...and I bet
By the cracking of dawning, the early morning
We still on and cracking, no yawning
Just pawning...I'm coming for you queen as you come at this King
This love thing...brings...out the best
This ain't Checkers but Chess
Checkmate...is your breasts
Winner takes all that's left...'Cause we going for the...
Championship
Peep the manuscript
You play the damsel in distress
No...You play the damsel in this stress
To help bring me out this mess
And I'm that Superhero lover that needs no rest
From your toes to the crease of your thighs I bless
Holding your heart is one of my many conquests
'Cause we're going for the championship
For better grip, let me grab your hips and guide you away

As we ride away, to my hide-a-way
In the tropics…and let's discuss topics
Of who's the top pick
I, the one and you, the two
Or I, the two and you're the one
Our road to the championship has just begun
But…you're…running the wrong way
This is training camp
I need you soft and damp
But you're running the wrong play
This here's Team Sun Ray
Where we join our lights so bright in sight
that no one stands in our way
So I say on this day
Without any malfeasance or treason
Let's stand before God and give Him a reason
To send down his blessings and bring fruit this season
With all that being said, I have nothing more to say
But I'd like to know…Where will you be on Game day?

Championship is one of my favorite love pieces. It really brings to light the concrete battle men and women face that hopefully culminates in the championship of love. I watch a lot of sports but football is by far my favorite. From Florida Gator football on Saturdays to Miami Dolphins' games on Sunday, I'm glued to my television during the season. It's the only time of year when men gleefully flee the company of their companions for the gratitude of the gridiron. The journey of love exemplifies this very same encounter. Athletic teams compete for MVP honors, championship rings, and trophies. Couples compete for leadership, life lessons, and God's blessings, in hopes to receive championship wedding rings. Singer Lauryn Hill croons in her ballad *Ex-Factor* that "love is a battle and we both end up with scars." However at the end of that battle is a level of intimacy that can lead couples to and through problems that many people cannot face or survive alone. I've always believed that in a relationship, one must relate to the ship or there can be no journey. The journey through the season to the championship is a long grueling one. I hope the one I choose has the wherewithal to make it out of training camp.

Contagious

In the midst of the moans and screams
This plan unraveled from the seams
Beneath the sounds of screams and moans
The ignition cut…we were not alone
What started as a bunch of "damn you fines"
Has led to my hands around her waistline
The tattoos on her neck get pecks
As Goosebumps travel down her spine
Running my fingers through her number nine
I'm pulling out my best lines
It's around this time; I missed the door shut
My ears sensed fears but my eyes see big butt
And a thigh so sly it jumped out to say hi
Taking any shy away from this guy
She rips off my tie; Saying that she wants it
Floors creak as faucet leaks, got me thinking house haunted
As this story builds with anticipation
Her clothes gain more emancipation
Feeling our hearts palpation
I take a moment to notice God's creation
Soft kisses and well wishes set the mood in motion
Intoxication from her love potion
Turns the wheels of my locomotion
I'm moving in a loco motion
Until I get distracted by the outside commotion
She says don't stop

Footsteps grow closer as my heart drop
She may be the cream of the crop
But nothing to lose my life for
Don't know what's on the other side of that door
But on this side she creams for more and more
She says give it to me baby
I give it to her…definitely, maybe
Lady, you're crazy
Back bent and love scents
Got this room so hazy; I can't see
Bladder fills when I'm nervous; I gotta pee
The door flies open
Frightened by what awaits me
I bear witness to the unfolding drama
This lil' nigga runs in yelling GET OFF MY MAMA!!!

I've always attracted and been attracted to older women. I don't know what sparks the attraction but I've rarely dated women my own age. Comedian Paul Mooney says that it starts in the classroom. I'd be willing to take his position because I've had my fair share of absolutely gorgeous teachers, professors, and school counselors. As a matter of fact, my seventh grade English teacher was the spitting image of Pam Grier. PTA meetings at this time were heavily attended. Fathers, uncles, and cousins would come out of the woodwork to "check on" their child in her class. Dating older women can be risky at times. One of those risks was depicted in this poem. Inspiration for my pieces can come from the strangest places. As I traveled down I-65 in Birmingham one morning, the Isley Brothers' *Contagious* streamed soothingly through the local R&B radio station's airwaves. It had been quite awhile since I'd last heard that hit. The video for the song granted music fans one of the most memorable narratives ever depicted on the Top 10 countdown. A younger man played by R. Kelly gets romantically involved with an older woman played by Chante Moore. Viewers later find out that the older woman is the wife of Mr. Big played by Ron Isley. The video reminded me of a similar situation I encountered. However, the heroin in my tale was no longer married. My encounter with Mr. Big was her very perturbed young son.

Breaking Up

This played out like your favorite shows episode
Her pain was like cancer spreading to the lymph nodes
Dying slow with no room to grow
Be careful of the seeds you sew
Cause she was gonna explode
But any longer and I would implode
I know absence makes the heart grow fonder
But it made mine wander
So I decided to go up yonder and visit my King
To see if a burning bush would reveal my queen
With which I would place this ring
To this the I'd wed and not this the bed
Yes, this relationship had legs
But long distance grew a wedge that we could not shed
And if He fed 5,000 with 5 loaves of bread
I knew he wouldn't leave her for dead
So to the sky I fled

This was a very hard poem to write. I hated the circumstances that created this piece. Towards the end of my college career, I met the woman of my dreams. I asked God for her and he answered my prayers. We were both new to relationships. I'd dated a few young ladies without any success. With her, I was her first boyfriend. We were both granted an opportunity to grow together. However, our relationship became difficult once I moved away. A lot of what we tried to accomplish fell short in the end. We were everybody's favorite couple. Upholding that image became a greater challenge than the relationship itself. We were two people of great faith that had ventured far away from the purpose in which we were placed together. The only remedy to the situation was to separate. It was hard. It was one of the toughest decisions in my life. But if Jesus "fed 5,000 with 5 loaves of bread, I knew he wouldn't leave her for dead."

Loved and Lost

Ok I get it you're serious
But now I get it I'm delirious
Loco, my membranes insane
Locked into a battle between the heart and the brain,
Its inane, the opposite of mundane
I pray this poem is not too late or in vain
Popular demand commands that I go against the grain
But the heart of this Lion instructs me to remove the stain
See I've been to the forest to live amongst the trees
And realize I'm nothing in the midst of the breeze which leaves
My heart withered my brain prevailed
My heart heard your cries
But it was enclosed in a cell
However, Love does not fail
Love has survived for centuries and lived to tell its tale
For it was love that drove a carpenter to overcome the world's hell
And if He can live and die by wood and nails
Then I'm gonna chart out a new course of which to set sail
And the tools at my disposal are words unfettered
And tell you that I'm sorry in hopes that it will make things better
But if it's too late and there's no room for 2nd chances
And you've allowed your sun to set
And your twilight begins to dance its dances
I'm sure you've grabbed your bags
And collected your sorrow
But before you turn your back to face tomorrow

I ask that you take those brown eyes, the same ones filled with pain
Join my hand again and go against the grain
Look deep within the confines of a mirror
And realize, please realize that your heart
and my heart need to be nearer
There's none I hold dearer
Let me make it more clearer
Simple and plain
I've weathered the storm
Pressed through the rain
I've fought the battle and conquered the beast within
Now how can I put you and I back together again

Ok, ok, I know what you're about to say. This makes my previous piece *Break'n Up*, totally obsolete. But I told you it was a difficult decision. The separation anxiety was too much to bear. This is the type of poem that will get your windows busted if you're not careful! This feeds into the "men ain't shit" philosophy that some women have. I didn't care! I had these feelings on my heart and I had to get them out! My soul was crying out. By expressing these feelings, I felt it would be therapeutic. However, it only made matters worse! There are points in this piece where I'm crying in a literal sense. When I state "please realize your heart and my heart need to be nearer," I had reached a point of no return. There were some things that I had to work on if I was going to be that king that every woman craves and deserves from their mates.

Love's Assassin

I couldn't let her heart heal
Cause I heart steal
I'm a heart thief
And the rest of her body I had beef
Which is why I heat..it up, eat it up, beat it up, and then switch sides
But that heart I stole
As if the game was on the line
And I was rounding 3rd base
And shot the umpire in the face cause he didn't say safe
Loud enough to deafen ears
So now he screamin' where everybody hears
Don't confuse this story with one of greed
This is the documentary of one assassin's creed
Some assassins use knives to take lives
Use guns on the run
But I've killed a countless thirds with one simple verb
Many have copied and borrowed from me
Very authentically I step to she and tell her I'm sorry
And it kills her softly cause she loved hardly
But I loved hardly ever
Depended on the weather
When I made it rain she took shelter, I felt her
Now I'm standing here the opposite of together
Holding her heart trying to keep it together
Cause I shattered it in tiny little pieces
She was a delicate species

You think I cared, I'm an assassin
But now I feel compassion
Distant memories of passion
I hope this pain is not everlasting
Cause I will unsheathe this sword and commence to blasting
On myself, maybe I should combine this heart to add health
Or spread it out to use it as a blanket
Because I'm cold in the midst of record highs

This is another great piece and true story written from an aesthetic perspective. This poem was inspired by a video game called Assassin's Creed. My poetic inspiration is limitless. Set during the time of The Crusades, the main character was assigned to collect information on various high profile targets. Once enough information was gathered he was ordered to them. The more I got into the missions associated with this game the more I noticed the similarities it had to man's quest for love. Not saying we set out to kill women. I'm definitely not promoting that. However, we do set out on conquests i.e. parties or any social gatherings, to accomplish the enviable yet daunting task of getting the contact information of a pretty young lady in hopes of getting to know her on a deeper level other than her physical appearance. On the assassin's journey he came across a target that revealed a truth in him that could not lie. This target's revelation altered the course of the main character. This sudden awakening caused an immediate personal inflection to take place. In the quest for companionship, there's always one who we meet that leaves a lasting impact that cannot be shaken. In this piece, the character felt life had become too predictable and sought to manipulate his path's practicality. Soon, he found out his power wasn't unconquerable. His outlook changed once he became the target. He devolved to a level of remorse. He was forced to utter the three toughest words in the English language, "I am sorry." What was more difficult than speaking those words was the fact his pride took a lethal blow. His pride was in his work and he was good at his job. Now that his job has been irreparably damaged, he's forced to start over and begin anew. Let's hope his latest endeavor finds him more humble and astute of his surroundings.

Pray For H.E.R.

I asked that He be a lamp unto my feet
And a light unto my path
He decided to go that extra mile
And do a little math
By assembling a crew of two he added you
He subtracted an unfaithful few
And became a painter
That turned my gray skies blue
The infinite, intrinsic, divinely artistic
The task of finding you
was made so simplistic
The swipe of His brush
Would make you blush
He cleared out a path
that lead to my crush
I was almost one of those pretentious guys
That was before I looked into your eyes
I know we've given this love thing several tries
But before you let your sun set
Allow me to let it rise.

Living in Tallahassee, FL would be a drag sometimes. To pass the time, I'd regularly attend this Monday night talent showcase at a place called *Amen-Ra's Bookstore*. Everyone from poets, rappers, musicians, singers, and comedians, would come out to entertain the eagerly anticipating crowd. While there, I met this singer who sang back up for

George Clinton and the Parliament Funkadelics. She had an amazing voice and incredible stage presence. She sang this original track one night that resonated with my spirit. It had a very jazzy N'awlins flavor to it. For the next few weeks I couldn't get this song out of my head. When I saw her again I told her that I would write a piece to her phenomenal track. She thought it would be a good idea and suggested that we perform it the following Monday. So I sat down to write *Pray for H.E.R.* It was an easy poem to write but it was so difficult to remember and perform. Throughout the week, I practiced this poem over and over, but I just couldn't remember it for the life of me. Eventually, I got to a point where I felt comfortable to present it. When Showtime came, she stepped to the microphone and gave a commanding performance. She then gave me a stirring introduction and I stepped to the mic and forgot every word to the poem!! At that moment I longed for the nearest Southwest airline because I really wanted to get away as their slogan says. However, let's not allow what happened on stage take away from what happened on the page. *Pray for H.E.R.* stands for "His eventual revelation." It breaks a man's quest for companionship down to a spiritual level. Men are often blinded by the outward appearance of women and fail to take a subcutaneous journey. This is a critical oversight because we miss a golden opportunity to connect with God's plan. Reverend R.B. Holmes of the Bethel Missionary Baptist Church in Tallahassee, FL used to say men should ALWAYS pray. He's right because God wants to be involved in every aspect of our lives. We pray about everything else, so why not pray about your choice in companionship. He will eventually reveal to us a woman that is nurturing, caring, sophisticated, and spiritually capable of complimenting the gifts He instills all men. When God lights a fire under our feet and sends us on a path, we should follow it knowing that he has our best interest at heart. I'm glad I took the time out to *Pray for H.E.R.*

Sunshine's Goodnight
(The Morning)

As I tuck you in
We begin to be stuck again
I make amends that this will be the end
Until we do it all over again in the morning
A soft kiss goodnight
Will make the 'morrow feel just right
A gentle breeze ushers in
Can't wait to see you in the morning
Let's make this a new trend
You and I friend daring to dream again
A place where only few ascend
All for the prize of opening our eyes
To face the dawn
Of a raying Sun
I'm glad I was a praying Son
And not a preying one
'Cause you make me feel like number 1
When life gets cumbersome
I look for my 2
We make such a dynamic crew
That's no joke
I give you a playful poke
No Facebook

The Dream Team gleam
I love how your face look
Let's huddle up
To run this play
We gotta huddle up
For extra points
Pull the cover up
And let's cover up
After I kill it
There may be a police cover up
But my feelings for you
I can no longer cover up
Ok that's enough
I've tucked…you're in
Now I wait
And anticipate
As my heart palpates I concentrate
On how great
It will be
To see
You again
In the morning

Separation anxiety runs rampant through young couples. This piece pokes fun at the perils that sleep can cause when a man misses his lady. What's ironic is that he needs his sleep in order to sustain a healthy relationship with his woman. As a man, there's nothing greater than having a beautiful woman wake up next to you. It's a priceless precious fortune for her to awaken in security and comfortability. Whereas, *"Let Me Hold You,"* conjures up images of a couple in a hammock, this piece clearly conceptualizes cuddle time cut short by rest. A night of romance capped off by intertwined intersected bodies can properly set a great nights rest in order. A night in life encapsulated by passion only leads to an overflow of emotions that creates a rift between rest and relaxation. This man displayed sentiment and passion that may seem foreign to our accompanying species. Many women complain about a man's lack of emotion. I disagree. Men are very emotional. With this piece I wanted to show women how emotional we can truly be. When you strike the right chords in us we become upright and steadfast in our journey to complement you which subsequently completes us. I know I can't live without you. So "let me hold you tight" as "I wait and anticipate the morning."

Waiting

(Sing) I'm waiting, waiting, waiting for the world to change
I'm waiting, waiting for this girl change

Into something revealing
Cause she's very appealing

To the eye of this guy
I try, to always be fly

So I check her back for wings
Cause I don't have time for flings

I'm after rings and I'm going a circle
I'm after a Win-slow like Steve Urkel

And I've never been higher than this altitude
For us to fly in formation it takes the right attitude

And I'll be there right by your side like a kidney
And we can jet off to places like Sydney,
Monaco, or I take you down to Tallahassee
Let's get our freedom on like Haile Selassie
Jamaican me crazy
Let's practice you making me babies
Our love is high so our love scent is hazy
You heard what I said

I take you back to the days when I was rocking dreads
And give you all the TLC cause I ain't too proud to beg
(Sing) See I'm waiting, waiting for the girl to change
But that's like waiting, waiting for this world to change
Her thoughts, her mind
You don't have to be defined by the design of your behind
But you don't know that cause you've been led by the blind
Been treated as 10 pennies instead of one fine dime
So join me in my upward climb
To see what treasures in heaven we can find
Trust me, I understand your hesitation
So until it's time to meet the needs of this reservation
Baby, I'll be here waiting….

After all the difficulties of my past relationships, I felt it was necessary to dream beyond a place of my existence. I wanted to dream of the perfect woman and the perfect relationship, including the flaws. I was in Old Navy and John Mayer's Waiting on the World to Change played over the loudspeaker as I walked past the dressing room. I watched this beautiful goddess step in to try on a pair of denim jeans, subsequently triggering my thoughts to write this piece. I immediately started typing into my blackberry and I came up with this piece. When Keenan Ivory Wayans would have staff meetings for In Living Color, he would always say to the cast and crew to find the funny. Well I've adopted a similar mantra called "find the flyness." When I "check her back for wings," I'm looking for that one specific gift that sets her apart from other women. That one specific gift is the gift of flight. Meet me in the clouds!

I Go Through It, Sometimes!

We Must Become Firemen

Here we stand as the great debaters, anticipators, articulators,
Innovators, motivators, caretakers, earth shakers
Color of the equator, image of the creator, inventors of everything
From the refrigerator to the elevator
An elevated mind state, whole armor of
God, check out my breastplate
A talented tenth indeed, but we find ourselves
in desperate need of firemen
People, We Must Become Firemen
To integrate this burning house and inspire men without tiring
Because where two or three are gathered, He'll be in the midst
So let's ban together and turn this fire into mist
Even though the devil will be pissed, the battle is not his
This done for the generations of kids, whose
life has love and whose eyes are hid
From this timeless devil that we've got on the ropes
So grab your hose and let's shoulder the load
As we put out the flames of poverty, prejudice, animosity and anger
Because we've never been a stranger to danger
Always broke laws for the cause
So let us take a rebel pause to examine our flaws to ask
Are you a fireman?
Are you someone worth admiring?
Can you run this race without tiring?
Because the situations we're facing dictate your hiring!

57

We Must Become Firemen is one of the most important pieces of literature dedicated to the civil rights struggle. Coming from Birmingham, AL, I've always had an eye towards the conquests of the future while not forgetting the contests of the past. I wrote this piece in January of 2008 while sitting in Wednesday night prayer service. The pastor had just seen *The Great Debaters* starring Denzel Washington. I hadn't seen it yet. He talked about it so much until I went to see it the next day. When you hear the line, "Here we stand as the Great Debaters," it's actually a nod to the sermon I heard that Wednesday night. This piece was inspired by a conversation between Dr. Martin Luther King, Jr. and Harry Belafonte. On the final episode of Tavis Smiley's NPR radio program, he played an interview with Harry Belafonte. Mr. Belafonte recalled one of his memorable moments with Dr. King in which they discussed at length the topic of integration. In that conversation, Belafonte asked whether integration was a good thing, and King responded that it was not so much whether integration was bad, it was what we were integrating into. We integrated into a burning house and we must become firemen. This is the challenge issued to Black people in 21st century America. We are often confronted with obstacles that uniquely effect people of color. God teaches us in the 6th chapter of Ephesians that we must put on the whole armor of God to withstand the wiles of the devil. If you take time out to read that whole chapter you'll find that Paul identifies an enemy in the devil, shows us the equipment we need to defeat the devil, and he explains the energy source that prayer provides to accomplish this task. Paul's address to the Church of Ephesus was written while he was in prison. The man that inspired this piece also wrote a letter, the infamous *Letter from the Birmingham Jail*, laying the ground work for today's fireman. Dr. King enlightens us on why Blacks cannot wait for whites to see the effects of segregation. He teaches that forcing the issue will bring about the change we need. Fast forward to today's challenges and you'll find the same burning houses. We must unite and put out the flames of segregation, high gas prices, dismal economic conditions, prejudices, poverty, animosity, and anger. The Bible also says that God has not given us the spirit of fear, but of power, love, and a sound mind. No other figure in American history exemplified these words better than the honorable Martin Luther King Jr. Let's not allow the message of the man to die with the messenger. We must become firemen.

2 Weeks Notice

Words cannot describe how much I hate you
You are the living embodiment of what I've failed to become
In my quest for number one
You are an obstacle that maybe fun for some
Not me
I detest you with glee quite passionately
No longer am I afraid to say this to your face
I'd gladly catch a case before becoming your corporate straight lace
Don't send any offerings to this pulpit
No need for a religious text to speak on this bullshit
Now that's pure!
For low wage you ask that I endure
Coffee lines no coffee cups
Healthcare with hiccups
Harassing hairy big butts
Is not the life for BStuc
I haven't even used my exceptional ability
The Internet says they make more in a correctional facility
This moment of clarity
Shouldn't be met with any sentiment of charity
However, this declarity should show just
how unbearably you are to me
I'm sick of the convos with coworkers of how you jerk us
I'm tired of the game with the office lame
Whose job it is to spy
They're the ones without lives

That simply goes home and cry
The truth is hard and a bitter pill
Yet we're forced to swallow
The worst day is payday when you leave my check so hollow
There are no winners only losers
Abusers, confusers, and missusers
I've done my time of nickel and dime
Being a servant to the intruders
Looking deep within this crystal
Seeing the grip you have on my balls
My soul cries out, I must leave these office walls
Shedding my final tear no longer will I sob
Let me clear my throat and say
"F*** YOU AND THIS JOB!!!"
Make sure you post it
And be sure to quote this
This…is…my…2…weeks…notice!

When the "recession" hit, new terms such as under-employed entered the American lexicon. Many companies forced highly qualified and highly skilled employees out of the door in an effort to save the bottom line. Companies crafted nuclear options to blindside unsuspecting employees with the news that their services would no longer be needed. These workers searched for employment in any way, shape, or form. I've heard the craziest, most gut wrenching stories that would temper the gentlest heart. People with master's and doctorate degrees were forced to obtain jobs of unequal skill sets to their educational background. This is why under-employment permeated the American airwaves. I know if I could speak for those individuals, their last spoken words would be the ones in this poem. I had a job at a place that I hesitate to label as a news organization considering that the people in positions of power did not have television backgrounds. Daily, I hummed the words to a song called "Spaceship" by Kanye West. In the song, he dreamed of acquiring a spaceship to lead him out of the daily rigors of his job. If there were such a thing as hip-hop, negro spirituals, this song would be at the top of the list. Now for those of you out there, who haven't worked in television news, know that it's a very dangerous place to be. The newsroom can be a place where even God cannot penetrate. I often felt like my prayers of another job were not being answered as long as I worked in such a hellacious environment. Friends that were once bright eyed and bushy tailed could no longer identify who they were and what they wanted to accomplish besides today's late breaking news story. I dated a reporter who worked with me at this television station. She was a classic tale of an employment opportunity gone terribly wrong. She was wired 24/7! Her whole life became the next story. I felt really bad for her. She had a sense that keeping her job was more important than keeping her sanity. A huge story broke once and she couldn't wait to come home to tell me about it. Once she got home, her jet set mind frame began to take shape. Her mouth was moving faster than Superman and The Flash in a race! I would literally have to tell her to slow down, breathe, eat, and for God's sake go to sleep! That was when I realized that the newsroom had similarities to a crack corner. The size of the crack rock was determined by what happened on your block. They'd often get high off of their own supply. When I realized that working with and around a bunch of crack heads was not for me, I crafted these words as my escape. I hope this poetic piece captures the sentiment felt in Kanye West's classic ballad.

Episode III

Protect and Serve

The Roc boys were in the building that night
Oh what feeling, they feeling right
Yee'n even have 'ta bring ya paper out
They were dope boys of the year
Drinks were on the house
The night before his girl became his spouse
It was his time his moment to shine
A night set aside for fun and thrills
Turned into one of spinal chills
Because….The Cop boys were in the building that night
Fresh off the beating of a beautiful wife
He needed a place to get his frustration out
The dope boys were nearby
Let's punch 'em in the mouth….
Police brutality brings about the brutal reality
Of the fallacy in the system
That dissed 'em
Dismissed 'em
As crazed and derange
Written off as pocket change in the grand scheme of thangs
While they stick their fangs
Deep within your flesh
Let me suck your blood
Til there ain't none left
And leave their communities bereft
Of role models

So they'll never grow to become Rhodes Scholars
Keep 'em as babies
Keep 'em as maybes
Keep 'em from their full potential
For it's essential,
To the plan
Of keeping a black boy
From becoming a black man
Make one an example
Make his blood flow ample
And if another gets out of line
Give 'em a sample of our injustice
Like an unjust kiss
Leave 'em real pissed
While the same laws slap us on the wrist
For them, go buck wild
Tell 'em they fit the profile of exile
Pay 'em 2 cents to make textile
Detach father from child
Turn man, brother, son, into child
And peep their motherless smile
As they cower to the power of the devour
Seeking to destroy Abner Louima, Jena 6,
These old tricks claimed the lives of Sean Bell
Who'd just begun with his story to tell
Timothy Thomas, Amadou Diallo,
And I'm sure there's more to follow
Protect and Serve
Those that have a gun
And if you're Black in America run

Like sitting still was a sin
Like standing idle was a trend that's no longer in
Get on the good foot and brake fast like the wind
Though we have the ability
To move through this life with such agility
With temperance and humility
In a world that lacks civility and decent human dignity

Too many times have I sat by and watched innocent African Americans fall victim to overzealous, pompous, police officers. Don't get me wrong. I'm not opposed to law enforcement serving their actual purpose. But catch the real bad guys. Catch the guy that's raping underage school children. Catch the guy that beats women. Don't catch and shoot the guy that's reaching for his wallet. Don't impale the guy's head that has a medical condition. Mistaken identity, prejudices, animosity, bitterness, and the inability to properly assess impending situations by the police have led us to this point in American history. Jay-Z's video for the hit single "Roc Boys" featured a celebratory extravaganza complete with beautiful women, celebrity appearances, top shelf liquor, and the widest smiles abound. However, the festive occasion ended in a tragic shootout. Although, the reason for the shooting depicted in the video was different, the motive was the same in the Sean Bell incident. This young brother and I were the same age. His shooting hit home in a lot of different ways. He was less than 24 hours away from marrying his fiancé. He was a father. He was a working man. He was everything opposite of the stereotype preceding him. While cornered by plain clothes police officers outside a New York City night club, he was met with a barrage of bullets that ended his life tragically, tumultuously, and unfortunately typically. I was too young to be socially aware of the brevity of the Rodney King verdict. However, looking back through the eyes of the Sean Bell tragedy, I understand that being young and black is to be under constant attack. I was inspired to write this piece while watching the aftermath of the Bell tragedy. The initial impetus came while on tour with Black on Black Rhyme in October of 2008. We were in Cincinnati, not too far from the University of Cincinnati, where I saw a man shake his head feverishly at the unwanted presence of the local law enforcement. "They all gon' burn 'n hell," he murmured. "There's a special place for all of them." I sought to engage this man in regards to his negative stance towards law enforcement. He began to tell me the story of Timothy Thomas, a 19-year old kid murdered by a Cincinnati police officer in April of 2001 sparking riots all over the city. Thomas was the fifteenth African American man killed by the Cincinnati Police Department in five years. After a brief foot chase, the arresting officer claimed Timothy reached for a weapon and he fired a fatal shot to the chest that ended his life. It was later discovered that he was unarmed and actually was in the act of pulling his pants up. "Damn bastard ass cop," he exclaimed, "he ain't hav'ta kill dat boy." I've tried to do all the right things in my life. I've stayed out of trouble and finished college. I haven't participated in gang activity, nor will you find children across the country with my DNA. Yet, I feel no different than a man who's serving a 25 to life sentence. These freedoms that I desperately seek can be taken away at any given time. Not from some haphazard circumstance, but from a mere misunderstanding. What will happen if I'm in front of a cop and I reach for my wallet in a manner that's misinterpreted by him? What happens if I'm locked out of the residence that I own and force my way in and I get harassed by local police as displayed in the Henry Louis Gates incident. If the Atlanta police department can break into an innocent elderly woman's home, shoot her and plant marijuana on her to justify the shooting like they did Kathryn Johnston, what will stop the same thing from happening to me. I pray for freedom, but freedom is certainly not free. I'll leave you with this:

> "No negro leaders have fought for civil rights, they paid for civil rights. They have begged the white man for civil rights. They have begged the white man for freedom and anytime you beg another man to set you free, you will never be free. Freedom is something you have to do for yourselves. Until the American negro lets the white man know that we are really, really, ready and willing to pay the price that is necessary for freedom, our people will always be walking around and second class citizens or what you call twentieth century slaves. The price of freedom is death. –Malcolm X

The Lion's Den

Your weak tactics don't faze me
You thought that you could haze me
The bullets you shot grazed me
For assassins y'all are lazy
And your actions are treasons
There's no chink in my armor 'cause I've read Ephesians
I'm the experienced candidate, I voted for change
I prayed for victory over the crazed and deranged
Y'all were rooting for me to fail but He's rooting for me to prevail
I'm more than a conqueror because he conquered hell
Torch fire, pitchforks, and brimstone
All come my way until I grab my phone
Because He's on the main line and I tell Him what I want
Praying to Him at night so that my dreams won't haunt
See I serve a living King so I'm something like a Fresh Prince
I Am Legend and I don't have to convince
Do your research, my family's royal
And when you do a drive-by, make sure you check your oil
And the guns that you used had no recoil
And the food that you ate was undercooked and spoiled
So it leaves you in a shitty mess
In a shitty car, with shitty guns, under distress
This is what happens when you contest my conquests
Used and abused and thrown in with the rest
While my day is filled with multiple Amens and God Bless
I stand on this mic and recite about my success

I should have named this piece "My Saving Grace" because that's what this piece became. The more I seek footing in this crazy world of ours the more that crazy world seeks to shakeup my footstep. I was working at a very stressful job at the time. The job was fun while it lasted but the people that worked there made it very painful. Every few weeks or so, "the powers that be" would select the name of an employee and make that person's life a living hell. One particular week my name came up. I was in a camera control room diligently recording a meeting on the changes in education requirements for teachers and administrators in the state of Florida. My supervisor was out of town and I was an hour or so into the meeting when I got a disturbing call over the PA system. "Wake up Brandan," a shrieking voice bellowed. "You better pay more attention to this meeting or else," the angry voice continued. I was caught off guard because out of the hundreds of meetings I covered during my tenure, I actually found this one quite interesting. The blind-side approach was one of their many tactics to bring about the demise of your employment. It only made them angrier when you wouldn't admit any wrongdoing. They would time their attacks around the time that my boss was out of town so upon his return he would be forced to take their side and reprimand any malfeasance. "I can't pay any more attention than I'm already giving" I cynically replied. With that simple line, I found myself at the angst of every member of management employed there. In adverse times such as this one, it is not in our best interest to take on our own problems. However, we must realize that there is a savior in the midst of turmoil named Jesus Christ. His duty in every believer's life is to shoulder the load that we cannot carry. Our duty as a believer in his word is to cast our cares on him, trust, and never doubt His ability to perform supernatural blessings in our lives. There are prevailing and demonic forces that seek to detain, denounce, and deconstruct the aspirations and ambitions laid before your path. I was raised in the church. My teachings have been to allow God to fight your battles. For that is the way to achieve ultimate victory. So with that logic, I've always approached adverse situations with the full armor of God. Those forces I mentioned have and will continue to seek your demise. However, God has a vested interest in your success. The line "Y'all were rooting for me to fail, but He's rooting for me to prevail, I'm more than a conqueror because He conquered Hell," should give you strength and comfort that no matter the outcome of your challenge, you've already received the victory.

At The End Of The Day
(Love vs. Money)

At the end of the day it was all about money
People do strange things for love
Money even stranger
Love will keep you safe
Money will put you in danger
Love is a want
Money is a need
Love will make you hurt
Money will make you bleed
Love is hate
Money is broke
Love is deep
Money is a joke
Love is open
Money is shy
Love will make you smile
Money will make you cry
Love will make a call
Money has gall
Love can withstand
Money can be your downfall
No matter what path in life you choose
Money comes first
Love will always lose

What happens when an unstoppable force meets an immovable object? That's the best description of the age old battle between love and money. I love performing but sometimes the money isn't there. Do I quit? He has a job that pays a lot of money but doesn't love the work. Does he quit? Her job pays well but she continues to search for love in a seemingly loveless world. Does she give up? A young couple is deeply in love with each other but lack the sufficient economical supply to sustain a marriage and start a family. Do they remit in their faithful pursuit? The answer to these questions is hanging by a small thread at the outcome of the Love vs. Money battle. Historically money has prevailed. Money can derail hopes and dreams and at the same time provide a means to facilitate dreams. I had a friend in college that majored in a field that paid very minimal on the front end but would pay more if he chose to stay on that path. Sensing mounting pressures from his family to be successful immediately, he gave up on his dreams and entered the workforce. This is a sad reality for most individuals. The victory will come by finding the silver lining that will provide a peaceful coexistence. The answer lies on the condition that a healthy balance develops between the two. One minute we want money the next we want love. Both are worth one's aspiration but are you willing to take that risk. My friend took a risk and cancelled his dreams. Sometimes it works in your favor and sometimes it doesn't. But at the end of the day everything comes full circle. The Bible says the love of money is the root of all evil. So does that mean the love of love is the root of all good? No. The two provide the same effect in people. The difference lies in the action. You have to do something for money. However love is free. At the end of the day, take a risk and choose a side.

"iGrow"

I praise His promise

I have patience in His preparation

I sing His Salvation

I seek His strength

I boast in His blessings

I bear witness to His breakthrough

I ask for His armor

I await His awakening

I walk with His worship

I run in His recognition

I follow in His footsteps

I prevail in His probability

I gather in His grace

I grow in God

iGrow is a quick piece that intends to provide an early morning spiritual boost to people who are going through trials and tribulations. Daily I receive tons of emails from different friends and family featuring devotions, prayers, and scriptures that's supposed to help get you through the day. I feel a lot of the emails talk at you instead of to you. I sought to create a more personalized response that gave a more accurate account from a believer in the power of Christ. As a young Christian, I'm still in the developing stages of my faith. One of the goals I wanted to accomplish with this piece was to accurately reflect the God that dwells in me. In John 4:4 it says greater is He that is in me than he that is the world. The "I" used in each line of the piece is further accompanied by the "H" and "S" of His, illustrating that I rest and reside in Him who created me.

The Storm of 5/1/09

I've been lied on and spied on
My shoulders have been cried on
But I carry on leaving others to tarry on
I'm fighting for my life
Armed with a knife
That's lodged in my back
Satan's on the attack
His whole army is ashore
This story has been told many times like folklore
I'm wounded but not defeated
Sacked but not decleated
Before Satan's goal is completed
My defense I've repeated
I scream, I shout, I call out to my Savior
The enemy sees this as erratic behavior
They're thrown off, weakness exposed and blown off
Fret not cause they'll soon be cut off
On the brink of disaster, I still see no loss
Yes, My situation is grim
I look to the Hills and I calleth out to Him
Lord Have Mercy upon their souls
Conquer my enemy before they accomplish their goals
Though a host shall encamp round about me
You told me to trust you and never doubt me
This life is rough this road is hard
I've trudged and trudged and called for God

Every step I take is filled with mud
But I've been covered by my Savior's blood
And I've never seen the righteous forsaken
Nor His seed begging bread
His word is my weapon, used where led
And when that devil approaches with his eyes bright red
My Lord, my God sends me to bed
So I may have rest and not be stressed
While he shows my foes why he's the best
The god of death, despair, and decoy
Doesn't compare to my God with all power to deploy
He goes to work to cease my storm
He acts as a shield from danger and harm
He Lives! He Lives!
His Wisdom, His Knowledge, He gives!
Jesus walks with the college dropout
Or your favorite team's standout
Though today is filled with an abundance of sorrow
God wipes your tears so you can face tomorrow
Just before the Amen
I almost gave in
Looking down at my wounds
Caused my faith to cave in
But I'm stronger than that
If I just hold on
This tale of despair will be long gone
So I share my story
Of God's great glory
And throughout history
God claims the victory!

Everyone has a testimony of overcoming adversity. I've had my fair share of ups and downs. But few were tougher than the hardship expressed in *The Storm of 5/1/09*. One of the deacons at my church said the words in this piece were a mirror with an accurate reflection of the God that resides in me. There's an old saying that a lie makes it halfway around the world before the truth has a chance to put its pants on. No other adage can better describe the events of that day. The circumstances that surrounded the creation of this piece involved a lie that was told on me. This lie spiraled so far out of control that I almost lost my job over it. Situations like these require the help of someone who can go places where I cannot. God challenged my resolve. He wanted to know if I would be a pessimistic quitter or an optimistic winner. I screamed, shouted, and called out to my Savior. He heard my cry and made me victorious. In tough times, we must remember that our outlook will determine our outcome. I was always taught to lean and depend on Jesus. So when my situation looked dismal, I did what I've always done to be successful. "I looked to the hills and called out to Him." Sometimes adversity is God's way of telling us to slow down. We cannot move faster than God. I had to slow down and get God involved. Once He was on board, the victorious outcome could commence. Ultimately, I lost a friend and a lot of good nights of sleep. I hoped that the bosses at that job weren't as crazy as they advertised themselves to be but they were. Actually, they were crazier! That's why I place my hope in Him not them because He had the track record of being undefeated in adverse situations.

The Paternity Journey

One of the best storytellers in modern day was the late great Notorious B.I.G. On his song *Niggas Bleed*, Biggie proceeded to tell one of the most prolific stories in hip-hop history about a drug deal gone badly. He described everything so vividly that I felt like I was actually there. In honor of his dynamic ability I wrote this piece. Not to discuss narcotics but to put into proper context the oldest hallucinogen called love. The following piece is a three part epic about a young couple facing off against the rigors of this world. It reverses the stereotypes held by society that says women are nice and sweet and men are like snakes, snails and puppy dog tails. This piece explores the transformation of the woman into our canine counterparts and the man into a much maligned but conservative role.

Act I

Her mother did her best
Papa kept her off the pole
I her pursuit for the whole world
But she lost her own soul
A single black female addicted to retail
An accentuated back-tail
That was adored by black males and used for blackmail
To get the good sale
50% off 50% on
50% right 50% wrong
She was an introvert that fell for extroverts,
Pimps, players, and in some cases skirts
Cold showers for hours was her time to cry
Inward pride aside no longer could she lie
She saw the truth in his eye, the gleam of his dream
Unite and take flight the King with his Queen
But…she's…a jezebel standing with the final nail
Her tears that wail, fills pails that tip scales
She knew he wouldn't take this well
So she walks in the kitchen with the pace of a snail
And told him "Honey sit down, I have a story to tell"

Here's a young lady whose been given all the tools to succeed in a professional environment. However, those tools created a pervasive attitude that seemed counterproductive towards any personal relationship gains with the opposite sex. She longed for a life of wrong that just felt so right. She sought to embrace the material things in life that she was initially shielded from. However, the man she met and entered a relationship with longed desperately to bring her out of a deceptive fantasy and into a blissful reality. But he had his own issues going on. His woman's secrecy began to get the best of him. It didn't help that a notable quotable from a childhood friend disturbed him to no end. Despite his better judgment, his friend had his best interest at heart. His friend's rants about the perils of being a companion to this woman reached a boiling point. One of the things he said to him reverberated stoically as he sat there at his kitchen table listening to who he thought was his baby's mother deliver frightening news. Here's what his friend said.

Act II

Men lie
Women lie
And sometimes numbers do
When what you thought was one…turns out to be two
Now you got three, now you mad at she
When it should be you…you know those kids don't look like you
You're a different hue…that baby's light-
skinned and you're midnight blue
With stars in your eyes settling for a consolation prize
Blinded by thick thighs that tell lies
A story…told on almost every episode of Maury
I ain't here to steal yo' glory
I'm just telling the truth no matter how uncouth
It's sad you ain't a proud dad
Brenda's got a baby, while you…You have a maybe
This is a lesson in paternity
Word is…she ran through your whole fraternity
And your boys say "She's burning me!"
And you wanna make her yours for eternity?
This concerns me
You need to take back that ring and watch, and
whatever else you got that you may think is hot
Stack your chips, load your clips, 'cause this is
a fight that'll last longer than tonight
From courtships to court trips
No longer a commitment, MANNNNNNNNNN!!
that test came back 99.9% Not Yours!
So when men lie and women lie….check your numbers…..

83

How would you feel if a bombshell of this magnitude was dropped on you? He had time invested. He had money invested. He had a future invested. He was provided an opportunity to be an alive-beat father instead of a dead beat one. So many children long for their fathers. His case was different. He longed to be a father. He was the last of a dying breed. His pride and ego was destroyed in one fatal blow. How would you carry on? If he was your son, brother, nephew, cousin, what advice or strength would you give him? I'm not certain of the answer but in this moment of weakness he needed help. His heart had taken control of his mind. Any action at this point would be an ill-conceived emotional setback. Once he accepted the fact that her words were true, he dealt with it in an unforeseen and an unadvisable fashion.

Act III

After he found they weren't his
He's reduced to tears
Held his head in his hand as he faced his fears
His high school sweet...they'd been together for years
Reduced him to nothing in front of his peers
He endured the type of jeers that could end careers
The knives in his back felt like tribal spears
His homies tried to warn him but it fell on deaf ears
Now the sound he hears is that of Atropos shears
Speeding down the highway, his life is shifting gears
The objects in his mirror are closer than it appears
He wants to go straight but his pathway veers
Listening to 'Pac he sheds so many tears
He faces the end of three long years
He can't handle the pressure from his fam' and peers
As his pathway clears
He speeds off the cliff as the afterlife nears.

No matter how hard the truth is to handle, I'll take it any day over a lie. The truth is a one stop shop and a lie is continuous. I am an advocate for truth seeking and truth speaking. Had she told the truth in the beginning, my friend would still be alive; wounded, but alive nonetheless. Pain can cut deep. Unfortunately his pain meant death. The third sister of fate Atropos had her scissors in proper position to cut the strings of his life. He felt the only way to get back at her for her treachery was to end his life and place it on her conscious. This was a sad conclusion he reached. My friend allowed his problems to become bigger than his God so he chose death over eternal life. To help within your community to prevent suicide visit http://www.suicidepreventionlifeline.org/ or contact 1-800-273-TALK.

The Conclusion

Destined

by:

Brandan "BstucThaPoet" Stuckey

My thoughts are sporadic and far from tame
I'm destined for greatness without a claim to fame
As soon as it's found everyone will know my name
From the mountains to the 'burbs I stay on my game
I will not slip I will not fall
I give you a little or I give you my all
Either way you receive a whole
Your time with me is worth its weight in gold
I'm destined for greatness someway somehow
I often have visions of taking a bow
In front of the masses as they cheer and clap
Giving ladies hugs and fellas some dap
Cameras flashing, the media a-buzz
I'm standing there thinking 'bout what used 2 be and what was
When nobody wanted to give me shot
When I thought my talents would sit and rot
Now is the time to earn a lot
And take what's rightfully mine, my spot on top
I'm destined for greatness, fame, and glory
And just as I'm about to continue my story
The visions I have become disrupt
A new day begins, Time to wake up.

The journey that we're on is far from complete. I hope the thoughts and ideas in this document help take you one step toward the greatness that we all seek. Rather than provide the same cliché answers, when asked in high school to foretell my future in 10 years, I decided to write this poem. We are all destined for greatness in some way, shape, or form. We have to continuously strive for it. It gets hard to stay above the fray but your will to prevent failure is one key building block toward success. The Bible speaks of being in the world but not of the world. God is trying to tell us that he's aware of the struggles this life presents. He knows there will be ups and downs. His job is to handle those things that are of the world so we don't miss his blessings that are in the world. Our job is to enjoy every gift that He places before us. It can be an early morning sunrise's reflection off the dew on the bluegrasses of Kentucky or the sunset off of San Diego beach in California. God offers these gifts to us to let us know that we have a clean slate. Every time I step on stage, it's God reminding me of a clean slate. Placing God in the proper position of our lives guarantees greatness. The next time you're at a spoken word venue, know that the poet who speaks has a story of greatness. With a clean slate we can move forward and fulfill our destiny. We are destined for greatness because we are his children. It feels good to be a descendant of the creator of the universe. With Him we can dream a dream in a time that would not seem it could be possible. Before he jumped on President Obama's case, I had the pleasure of hearing a lecture by Tavis Smiley at Florida A&M University. In his speech, Tavis spoke about the small distance between the womb and the tomb. When we're born, we are delivered between feces and urine, an asshole and a urethra. The ground we are placed in after death are fertilized by those very same ingredients. Taking these parameters, it's no wonder that so many young Black men think about death i.e. the character in *Paternity Journey*. There's an overpowering sensation of a looming endgame prevailing over every step we take. Tupac often rapped about death being around the corner. Hip-hop music came from death or poverty which is a proverbial death. So many artist have a symbiotic success story filled with the synergy of the street life and overcoming the very same pious pitfalls. In essence, they reverse the cycle of death by rising from it and gaining new life through music. I challenge you to live for today. Live knowing that tomorrow is not promised. Live while the opportunity presents itself. Live like the aristocracy of your intellect supersedes the mendacity of the populous. In February of 2004, I cracked open the CD case of *The College Dropout*. This album would soon become the definitive album of a generation. Three years later, I shared backstage chat time with the author of that album, Kanye West, like we'd known each other for years. That was a dream of mine to meet one of my favorite artists. Mission accomplished. It was a dream of mine to write and publish a book of spoken word. Mission accomplished. So when your last words are spoken, I hope you speak a message of greatness because it is your destiny. Mission Accomplished!

Poetry and Spoken word are parts of the creative world of Brandan J. Stuckey. Stuckey's journey is true and powerful. Hailing from Birmingham, AL, Stuckey honed his craft on numerous microphones in the Civil Rights Capital. One of the greatest strengths of Stuckey's writing is his poetic development and his ability to transition seamlessly between each poem. "I serve a living King/So I'm something like a Fresh Prince/I am Legend and I dont have to convince," is one of the many soulful quoteables that you'll hear from him. He allows each poem to tell a story regarding each transformation in his life. Stuckey was inspired to become a poet after writing a piece for his high school black history month play. After a standing ovation from a crowded auditorium, he harnessed that energy and turned into a successful poetry career. Each piece will take the reader on an adventure and encourage a personal search for their own feelings of inspiration, triumph, relationship, victory, and spirituality. He says his elements of poetry include "the deepness of Langston Hughes, the storytelling of Notorius B.I.G., the sheer rhetorical genius of Outkast, and the comedic excellence of Jamie Foxx." Stuckey gives a new and different voice to the spoken and written words of poetry. You can catch him on a microphone near you!